WHEN GOD IS IN THE CLASSROOM

WHEN GOD IS IN THE CLASSROOM

A devotional to help Christians know deeper fellowship with Jesus as He beckons them to follow Him in the classroom.

LAURA ACKLEY & BRIANA WHISTLER

EQUIP PRESS

Colorado Springs

Library of Congress Control Number: 2022913728

First Edition: 2022
When God Is in the Classroom / Laura Ackley and Briana Whistler
Paperback ISBN: 978-1-958585-04-7
eBook ISBN: 978-1-958585-05-4

ENDORSEMENTS

The fact that the role of an educator is extremely challenging is not news to any educator. Laura Ackley and Briana Whistler have written an excellent devotional which serves to remind every teacher that they are not alone. God is ready and able to help them face the enormous challenges of education and make a difference in the lives of each of their students. *When God Is in the Classroom* will give you inspiration and power you need to face each day.

Pastor Rick Lamb, retired pastor of Northside Baptist
Church of Corsicana, TX

In a world of uncertainty and trials, *When God Is in the Classroom* is like a timely heart-to-heart with a deeply trusted friend; leaving you feeling refreshed and sharpened. I cannot think of a person to whom this book would not be applicable. It accurately and concisely guides you through some of the highs and lows of working with others while pointing you directly to Christ Jesus and helps you live as His followers.

Emily Smith, BSN, RN, children's ministry coordinator at
Central Baptist Church of Blooming Grove, TX

I found this devotional to be wonderful! I would have gifted this devotional book to the teachers on my campus in a heartbeat! This devotional book will inspire others daily to find great joy in teaching and to seriously focus on their responsibility to show the love of Christ to their students.

Amy Gibbs, retired principal and 3rd Grade teacher of
Corsicana, TX

This is it! The book I have been waiting for as a teacher and school counselor. With all the chaos and challenges facing educators today, this book gives Biblical solutions, examples, and tools to face many situations in your classroom when you are feeling overwhelmed. The passion for Christ in the classroom the authors share is contagious, and their wisdom for your classroom is life changing! Through stories, Bible verses, and shared experiences, you will feel His presence in your classroom."

Debbie Powers, school counselor of Sam Houston
Elementary of Corsicana, TX, College Professor at
Navarro College of Corsicana, TX

Briana and Laura have a way of presenting deep biblical truths in a relatable and accessible format. No matter what role you play in teaching others this study is going to keep you grounded and point you to Christ as it reminds you of your true purpose: to bring glory to God.

Tabitha Powell, Children's teacher at Frost Baptist
Church of Frost, TX

When God Is In The Classroom is a month-long devotional for educators, and can I just say, "Wow!" These daily devotionals are reminders that what we do as educators, every day, is good. He knew about the daily trials we would face even before He formed us in our mother's womb. Laura and Briana remind us that these babies are in our schools, in our classrooms, and in our lives for a reason. I encourage every educator to read each day with an open heart and see how God is working in your classroom and school. Dig into these scriptures and know that He created each one of us for this exact time. These devotionals are true blessings shared from two beautiful souls who love our Jesus with all their hearts.

Allyson King, Principal at Blooming Grove Elementary
School of Blooming Grove, TX

When God is in the Classroom focuses the teacher's attention on the selfless example of Jesus Christ and the difference Christ's love can make in the lives of their students. Its concise daily devotionals can be read a few minutes before the students enter the classroom, providing biblical truth and encouragement that will have an impact throughout the day.

Dr. Darren Heil, Head Pastor of Central Baptist Church
of Blooming Grove, TX

DEDICATION

We dedicate this devotional first and foremost to God, as it was written out of love for Him with the sole purpose of bringing glory to His name. Additionally, we dedicate this devotional to Christian teachers all over the world who humbly serve and love their students in the name of Jesus. May they know His presence in their classrooms!

TABLE OF CONTENTS

ACKNOWLEDGMENTS

We would like to begin by thanking our loving husbands, Scott and Drew, for praying with us and supporting us as we spent time writing this devotional. We love you both!

Most importantly, we would like to thank Jesus Christ, our absolute joy and prize in life! When our attitudes and actions have been less than godly, You have been patient with us as You reminded us of Your presence in the midst of our chaos. You have sustained us in our classrooms, and You have not discredited our attempts to honor You in writing this devotional. We are thankful that You are our ever-present help in the time of need. We are thankful that You helped us bring this devotional to completion. May Your name be glorified in all the earth.

INTRODUCTION
By: Laura Ackley

Briana Whistler and I have been close friends since our elementary school years. Our older sisters played on the same Little Dribbler's basketball team; therefore, we developed a relationship playing together while they attended practice. As time passed, we grew in our friendship as we celebrated each other's decisions for Christ, marriages, pregnancies, babies, homes, birthdays, and career accomplishments. We have been there for each other through loss and heartbreak, hospital stays and hard days. We have been accountability partners, prayer warriors, and served in ministry together at women's conferences and Vacation Bible Schools. We consider each other sisters in Christ and regularly thank God for our 24 years of friendship—an absolute gift of God's grace. Through it all we can attest to the truth, "a friend loves at all time, and a brother is born for a time of adversity" (Prov. 17:17)1.

Both Briana and I felt called by God to serve as educators and have a combined experience of 11 years in education. Although our timelines and areas of service are different, it was through our positions as teachers that we experienced the call of God on our lives to co-write a devotional designed for Christian teachers. Oh, and a little push from a few dear friends that clearly believe we do not already have enough on our plates. We deeply know the daily joys and challenges associated with working with young people, their families, administration, and co-workers. Teaching is not for the faint of heart. We have empathy and understanding for the challenges that teachers navigate day in and day out, year after year, for the sake of their students. In our biased opinions, teachers are the most selfless, inspiring people. They give freely without expecting anything in return, just like our Savior, Jesus Christ. We love teachers and believe they are truly the heroes of society.

As two teachers, we are convinced that Jesus makes all of the difference in the way we operate in the classroom. Nearness to His presence is our life-line. We long to see His Kingdom come on the earth and for His good and perfect will to be done in teachers' lives. We desire to see Him exalted

---

1   *ESV Study Bible: English Standard Version,* Wheaton, IL: Crossway, 2011.

in successes, and we long to see Him turned to in trials. He is the answer to our need, the supply to our lack, and our strength in weakness. We know from the Bible and our experiences that God is ever-present by nature and indwells each person that has surrendered the control of their lives to Jesus as their Savior and Lord. Due to these truths, God is in our classrooms. No doubt about it. He can never be removed. Because of this, we do not think of our inability to freely talk about Jesus as a hinderance in the public-school classroom; rather, we consider it an opportunity to let our every action be seasoned with the love and service of Christ as we remain in constant communication with Him and depend on His strength.

This devotional was designed out of our longing to see God glorified as Christian teachers live in awareness of God's presence in their classrooms. The goal of this devotional is to aide in equipping teachers of faith as they serve and love their students in the name of Jesus. We hope and pray that these daily devotions assist Christian teachers by redirecting their attention from the negative aspects of teaching to the incredible attributes of God and transforming truths from His Word. As teachers begin their days by dwelling on His Word, they are reminded of the implications of their union with Christ through God's Spirit as they seek to fulfill their roles in their classrooms. As they study the Scripture and read the devotions we've written, we pray that teachers are encouraged to look to Jesus, their ever-present help and the greatest Teacher to have ever walked the earth. Additionally, we hope that they are encouraged to put off behavior that is harmful to themselves and others in order to walk in the freedom of Christ's peace and joy throughout their day-to-day responsibilities. Through focusing attention on Christ through the use of *When God Is in the Classroom*, we desire to see teachers equipped and encouraged to not grow weary in their God-given responsibilities; rather, to remember that they are empowered by God's Spirit to be the hands and feet of Christ in their respective callings.

When God Is in the Classroom is a month-long devotional that provides readers with a daily memory verse, extended reading passages, a devotional thought, and application section per work day. This devotional is applicable to all varieties of teachers, including individuals preparing to become school teachers, Sunday school teachers, or home-school teachers. This devotional applies to educators' diverse classrooms including public schools, private schools, home school, and church classes. We believe that this devotional works best if used prior to carrying out one's responsibilities for the day.

God is ever-present, and He fills His people completely. These truths

---

By: Laura Ackley

are game-changes for Christian teachers. As you set aside a month to remember His presence in your classroom through use of this devotional, we pray that you will recall that you are partnered with God. Your loving actions, however small they might seem, make a difference in the lives of children. The things you do for your students (that are as natural and thoughtless as breathing) move the heart of God. As you lay down your life for your students and kneel down to serve your students, remember, God is in your classroom. The presence of God is in you, dear Christian teacher. Do not give up. Your God-given, servant-heart does not go unnoticed by the greatest Servant of all. He is with you. He is in your classroom. And when God is in the classroom, hearts and lives change for the better.

OUR EVER-PRESENT HELP
By: Laura Ackley

MEMORY VERSE: "God is our refuge and strength, a very present help in times of trouble" (Ps. 46:1).

EXTENDED READING: John 14:15-31, Galatians 5:16-26

It is hard to imagine how anything could be more advantageous than the physical presence of Jesus among His people, but Jesus said in conversation with His disciples that it was to their "advantage that [He] go away, for if [He] did not go away, the Helper [would] not come to [them]" (John 16:7). Jesus promised to send His infinite Spirit to indwell His followers so that they would not be left to their own devices while He was in Heaven. The Holy Spirit is more than just a mystical idea that gives us goosebumps; rather, the Holy Spirit is the third person of God. God is one entity who manifests Himself as three separate persons: Father, Son, and Holy Spirit. The Holy Spirit is sent to indwell a believer when they come to saving faith in Christ. When people hear and believe the Gospel of Jesus Christ and receive salvation, they are "sealed with the promised Holy Spirit, who is the guarantee of [their] inheritance" in Heaven (Eph. 1:13-14). It is a joy to the redeemed that the Holy Spirit lives inside them, but anyone who does not have the Spirit of Christ does not belong to Him (Rom. 8:9).

Jesus referred to the Holy Spirit as the Helper that God would send to His followers in the name of Jesus to teach them all things and bring to remembrance the words of Jesus at the necessary moments (John 14:26). Prior to the sending of the Holy Spirit, the Spirit of God would "rush upon" or "rest upon" people as they were empowered and equipped to accomplish incredible feats through the power of God, but the presence with them would not remain. Jesus explained that the Holy Spirit would indwell His followers and remain with them forever, providing them with constant access to all of His benefits (John 14:16), including the gifts and fruits of the Spirit. In addition, we rely on the Holy Spirit to bring comfort, guidance, direction, and remembrance of Jesus' words. The Holy Spirit is responsible for transforming a Christian into the image of Christ through the process of sanctification and empowers them to live out their God-given callings in life. In the Spirit, a believer is sealed into God's family forever. The Spirit provides connection with God at all times! As we consider the benefits of the Helper in our lives, we agree with Jesus' statement from John 16:7, it is to our advantage that Jesus ascended to Heaven because He sent His Spirit to be our constant companion throughout all of our days.

As we seek to love and serve Christ in our classrooms, we should remember that "the Spirit helps us in our weakness" (Rom. 8:26). He is the One who is closer than our skin; therefore, He is present in all we face in the workplace. This is no small thing. With the Holy Spirit, teachers and staff are able to operate in the power of God and bear fruit in their day-to-day activities. Since Christian teachers are indwelled by God Himself, He is in their classrooms. Tangibly. Beautifully. Teachers, hear the call of God to walk by the Spirit. Live by His Spirit. His presence makes all the difference.

APPLICATION: Read and list the fruits of the Spirit from Galatians 5:22-23. Circle three fruits that you feel like you are not producing in your classroom. Take time to pray about the lack of fruit in each of those specific areas. Mediate on the truth that when you focus on walking by the Spirit, you "will not gratify the desires of the flesh" (Gal. 5:16). Remember, the third person of God is in your classroom, today. Walk by Him.

By: Laura Ackley

GRACE THAT GIVES FREELY
By: Briana Whistler

MEMORY VERSE: "And God is able to make all grace abound to you, so that having all sufficiency in all things at all times, you may abound in every good work" (2 Corinthians 9:8).

EXTENDED READING: 2 Corinthians 12, Ephesians 2:10, Hebrews 12

Grace is something we do not deserve, yet it has been given to us regardless of our works. We see and experience it in many ways in our day-to-day lives, our relationships being one example, but the biggest example in which we behold grace is in our Savior, Jesus Christ. We did nothing to deserve His sacrifice, yet He willingly endured the cross on our behalf in order to offer us forgiveness of sins and eternal life. God gave us this grace at the cost of His Son's life. His sacrifice of being beaten and killed on a cross gave us the free gift of God's grace—that we wouldn't be separated from God due to our sins.

Not only does God give us this gift of Salvation, but He also gives us grace in little things throughout our lives. It's in the peace that passes over you during a struggle or the consequence you didn't receive because of a poorly thought-out choice. Grace is abundant in our lives because God has chosen to give it. He has given us such a gift so that we would lack for nothing. Paul told the church of Corinth that God's grace is sufficient (2 Cor. 12:9). It's because of this sufficient grace that God has given us that we can carry out His good works that He has planned for us each day (Eph. 2:10). These works include giving this same grace to others around us (Heb. 12:15).

When God is in the classroom, the grace by which He saved us through Christ is a gift, not to us alone, but also to those around us. We did nothing to earn this grace. Sometimes those around us do nothing to earn grace from us. Sometimes our emotions tell us to respond in pride, anger, fear, or embarrassment. Sometimes we are wronged, and we experience pain. But God tells us to give grace. Give what isn't deserved because Christ took what we deserved on the cross. That is amazing grace.

APPLICATION: Read Ephesians 2:1-10. Write down the ways in which God has given you grace. Read Ephesians 2:4-5. What attribute of God do you see here? Write the memory verse on a notecard. Keep it close and read it anytime you feel yourself being overwhelmed with emotion. God has given you all sufficiency to do this job!

GREAT IN HIS EYES

By: Laura Ackley

MEMORY VERSE: "Little children, let us not love in word or talk but in deed and in truth" (1 John 3:18).

EXTENDED READING: Matthew 25:31-46, Matthew 18:1-6

Toward the end of Jesus' ministry on the earth, Jesus taught His disciples about the final judgment to come in which all people would either be rewarded in His sight or face His condemnation. In His illustration, those that were eternally rewarded by Jesus were said to have provided Him with food, drink, and clothing. Jesus said that they had welcomed Him whenever He was a stranger and visited Him whenever He was sick and in prison. Confused, they asked, "when did we do these things, Lord?" To their questions, Jesus replied, "Truly, I say to you, as you did it to one of the least of these my brothers, you did it to me" (Matt. 25:40). Jesus considers the good, compassionate works that we do for others to be done directly to Himself.

There is much beauty and greatness to be found in the eyes of Christ whenever believers humble themselves and serve those in their care in the name of Jesus. Jesus addressed this idea whenever He explained how He measures greatness in the Kingdom of God. The "great" in the Kingdom of God aren't the popular, successful, rich, famous, influential, or powerful; rather, "whoever humbles himself like [a] child is the greatest in the Kingdom of Heaven" (Matt. 18:4). What do children have that we must possess in order to be considered great? They have dependence on the adults in their life, just as we are called to have dependence on Christ. This requires humility and willingness to admit our need for God. Simple acts done for children and co-workers in humility are considered great in the eyes of Christ. The greatest people, in His opinion, are the ones that seek to humbly serve in His name with childlike faith in Him.

Immediately after defining greatness, Jesus says "whoever receives one such child in My name receives Me" (Matt. 18:5). Each student, child, or person we welcome in the name of Christ, Jesus counts as a welcoming of Himself. As we humbly bend down to tie shoelaces in the name of Christ, we do so for Jesus. As we welcome a challenging student into our class and choose to speak respectfully to them, we welcome and speak kindly to Jesus. We are truly the hands and feet of Christ, but we are also called to serve Christ by doing humble acts of service while loving those in our path. What we do for the least, we do for Jesus. He is in our classrooms. Although good works do not earn for us entrance into the Kingdom of Heaven, we are called by God to love everyone in our lives "in deed" (1 John 3:18). True Salvation will be evidenced by humble works done out of love for Christ and love for others—even those that might be difficult to serve and love.

APPLICATION: Anytime you recognize in yourself a hesitancy to serve someone, consider what might be holding you back and write it down. Maybe the particular person rubs you the wrong way with their behavior or attitude? Whatever the case, say aloud, "I'm doing this for Jesus" as you write John 14:15 next to each situation. This will remind you to love out of obedience to Christ. When you find your heart growing hard toward a particular child or co-worker, ask for God's strength to view this fellow image-bearer as Jesus Himself. Then, serve the Lord with gladness.

OPERATING IN HIS STRENGTH FOR HIS GLORY

By: Briana Whistler

MEMORY VERSE: "But He said to me, My grace is sufficient for you, for My power is made perfect in weakness.' Therefore, I will boast all the more gladly of my weaknesses, so that the power of Christ may rest upon me" (2 Cor. 12:9).

EXTENDED READING: 2 Corinthians 12, Philippians 4:13, Psalm 18:32, Psalm 46:1

No one likes to speak of their weaknesses. Most people think they are strong and independent, and that they can accomplish anything they want. At least that is what the world will tell us. The truth is that we are all weak. In one area or another, we will all fail at some point. These failures tempt us to feel weak and upset. Sometimes anger is our go-to emotion because we didn't accomplish what we wanted to accomplish. This leads to a heart of idolatry. 1 Corinthians 10:13-14 tells us that "no temptation has overtaken you that is not common to man God is faithful. He will not allow you to be tempted beyond your ability, but with temptation He will provide a way of escape that you may be able to endure it. Therefore, my beloved flee from idolatry." As followers of Jesus, it is God's will for our lives to resist the temptation of seeing weakness as a problem. Instead, we should embrace it because that is when God's power is perfected in us.

Tribulations will come in life (John 16:33). We will have events that knock us down and make us shudder under pressure. We will feel as though

---

we have no strength. During these times, the only place to go is the cross. Any other place we go leads to a heart of idolatry and sinfulness. We bow down to the feet of our vices and comfort rather than kneeling at the feet of Jesus. We mustn't give in to what we are feeling; rather, we should see these feelings as a warning system for what is happening in our hearts. We trust God to strengthen us in our weaknesses. God gives us grace (Eph. 4:7). He has it already apportioned to us, and it is through grace that we are able to approach His Holy throne and seek refuge in Him.

When God is in the classroom, His present grace that He has given is sufficient for our every need. We do well to embrace our weaknesses and allow God's strength to carry us through each trial. In each meltdown, Christ is sufficient. In each confrontation with a coworker, Christ is sufficient. In each moment of disarray, Christ is sufficient. Being a child of God means that Christ's power rests on us to carry out every good work (2 Cor. 9:8).

APPLICATION: Your weakness is what gives you strength through Christ. Write our memory verse on a note card. Keep it with you and read it in your moments of weakness. Each time you experience a moment of weakness, write it down. At the end of your day, pray through your list and ask God to strengthen you each time you encounter these weaknesses.

THE GREAT TEACHER
By: Laura Ackley

MEMORY VERSE: "You call me Teacher and Lord, and you are right, for so I am" (John 13:13).

EXTENDED READING: John 3:1-36, John 13:1-20

The title *Rabbi* was assigned to leaders in the religion of Judaism. "Rabbi" is literally translated as either "my master" or "teacher." Although Jesus was not in temple leadership, He was often referred to as "rabbi" or "teacher" by His followers due to His teaching ministry. Undoubtedly Jesus had a reputation for being a great teacher. In fact, Jesus was addressed directly as "Teacher" two-thirds of time recorded in the Gospels. An actual Jewish leader, Nicodemus, referred to the seemingly uneducated Jewish man from the middle of nowhere as the "Teacher sent from God" (John 3:2). When Jesus taught, people were taken aback and totally astonished by His teachings! Why? Because Jesus taught the people "as one who had authority" (Matt. 7:28-29).

On the night He was betrayed, Jesus, the Great Teacher, took up the position of a servant and washed His disciples' feet. After doing what was unheard of by any teacher of authority, Jesus taught His students one of the most important lessons to date: "If I then, your Lord and Teacher, have washed your feet, you also ought to wash one another's feet" (John 13:14). Jesus set an example for His followers: teachers wash feet. Teachers after the heart of Jesus are willing to serve their students despite their higher position. Teachers operating through the power of the Holy Spirit teach their pupils to serve one another as well.

Today, we are called by the Rabbi to remember that He esteems teachers and carried the title of teacher Himself. In the classroom, when we are at our wits end and do not know what to do or how to respond, know that there is unrestrained access to the Great Teacher. He promises,

---

"If any of you lacks wisdom, let him ask God, who gives generously to all without reproach, and it will be given to him" (James 1:5). Jesus our Teacher longs to teach and guide us as we seek to wash the feet of those in our care. We are not left alone. The Great Teacher is with us. God is in our classrooms.

APPLICATION: Write down an area in which you long for the Great Teacher to instruct your heart. Maybe you don't know how to respond to a certain situation? Maybe you lack wisdom on how to help a child with a learning or behavior difficulty? Read Psalm 32:8. Write a prayer of thanksgiving knowing that the teaching and counsel of God is available to you.

GOD IS THE ULTIMATE AUTHORITY

By: Briana Whistler

MEMORY VERSE: "For by Him all things were created, in heaven and on earth, visible and invisible, whether thrones or dominions or rulers or authorities–all things were created through Him and for Him" (Col. 1:16).

EXTENDED READING: Psalm 103:19, 2 Corinthians 4

God is our ultimate authority. There are numerous scriptures that point to this truth. Paul told the Romans "Let every person be subject to the governing authorities. For there is no authority except from God, and those that exist have been instituted by God" (Rom. 13:1). Even our government has been given their authority by God, and therefore answer to God. He is the supreme power over all things on heaven and on earth (Ps. 103:19).

Not only is God our ultimate authority, but He also created all things "visible and invisible" (Rom. 13:1). Nothing was created by accident, and "the Lord has made everything for its purpose" (Prov. 16:4). If everything has a purpose, that includes us. God made us for Him. "For we are His workmanship, created in Christ Jesus for good works, which God prepared beforehand, that we should walk in them (Eph. 2:10), which means that in God's ultimate authority, He created us for a purpose that He has already established.

It can be difficult to remember that God is the ultimate authority in the classroom. There are many different challenges that tempt us to follow a different authority and live to please people: administration, parents, students, coworkers. All of these circumstances work together to keep us from putting God and His commands in the forefront of our mind. But

---

just as Peter and the apostles answered in Acts 5:29 "we must obey God rather than men." God is our ultimate authority. We will answer to Him on the day of judgment, and He will "bring every deed into judgment, with every secret thing, whether good or evil" (Ecc. 12:14). As you go about your day in the classroom, work under the knowledge that God is your authority, and He is working out His purposes through you.

APPLICATION: Read Romans 12:9-21. Write down each mark of a true Christian. God is our authority. When we submit ourselves under His authority we are subject to the marks of a true Christian. Next to each mark write out what these marks look like in your classroom. (Example: "Rejoice with those who rejoice." In the classroom, this could look like you encouraging and celebrating with your students in their victories).

GOD'S WORKMANSHIP
By: Laura Ackley

MEMORY VERSE: "For we are His workmanship, created in Christ Jesus for good works, which God prepared beforehand, that we should walk in them" (Eph. 2:10).

EXTENDED READING: Ephesians 2:8-10, Psalm 139:13-16, and James 2:14-17

You are a work of art. In Ephesians 2:10, the Apostle Paul declared that we are God's workmanship. The Greek word used for "workmanship" is a verb, *poieo*, from which we derive the English word for poetry. Yes, the idea of epic poetry is wrapped up in this word to describe our created essence. We are the poem of God, His beautiful workmanship. We are made in the image of God—His living masterpiece in which He declares as "very good" (Gen. 1:31). The idea of workmanship stretches beyond a simple created thing. On the contrary, workmanship speaks to the talent behind the Creator's handiwork. How beautiful it is to consider the fact that we aren't just created, but we are claimed as "His workmanship" along with the galaxies, ocean depths, forests, and mountains.

Additionally, when anyone comes to saving faith in Jesus Christ's atonement for their sins and commits their lives to following Him as their Lord, by His miraculous creative power that person is made a new creation in Christ (2 Cor. 5:17). They are created anew in Christ Jesus for divine purposes. The workmanship God exhibits in giving one new life in Christ is creative power that is both redemptive and sanctifying. As His workmanship we have purpose in the classroom, hallways, cafeteria, parking lot, and beyond.

In His foreknowledge God has predetermined good works for us to walk out. He knows exactly what He has given each person to do every day; therefore, each good work, however mundane or insignificant

---

it might feel, is exceedingly important to God. Although Christians are not saved by good works, their good works in the name of Christ are evidence of their conversion. In the classroom, remember, we are called to "maintain good works" (Titus 3:8), to "be doers of the Word" (James 1:22), and "be zealous for good works" (Titus 2:14). As we navigate the stress in our workplace, we must remember the words of our coming King, "Behold, I am coming quickly, and My reward is with Me to give to everyone one according to his work" (Rev. 22:12). As opportunities to step into good works present themselves, know that hard-work isn't just for the benefit of the children, but Jesus takes it personally as if you the good works were done directly to Him. Even in the most challenging circumstances, choose to work for the Lord, knowing that from Him, we will receive an inheritance as our reward for our good works in His name and for His glory (Col. 3:23-24).

APPLICATION: Today, bask in the truth that you are the poem of Christ, created in Him for good works! Briefly jot down several tasks you are required to do but do not enjoy. Next to each task, write down one of the following Scriptures: Galatians 6:9, 1 Corinthians 16:14, James 2:18, or Colossians 3:23-24. Commit to focusing your attention on loving Jesus through each work that you accomplish throughout your day. It moves His heart and fulfills His purposes.

By: Laura Ackley

COMFORT IN AFFLICTION
By: Briana Whistler

MEMORY VERSE: "Blessed be the God and Father of our Lord Jesus Christ, the Father of mercies and God of all comfort, who comforts us in all our affliction, so that we may be able to comfort those who are in any affliction, with the comfort with which we ourselves are comforted by God" (2 Cor. 1:3-4).

EXTENDED READING: Psalm 56, 1 Peter 2:21, 2 Corinthians 4:16-18

In this life we are promised affliction (John 16:33). Affliction is uncomfortable. At times, it can be excruciating, or even make us long for our heavenly home, as Paul wrote in 2 Corinthians 2:8-9. Affliction is usually not something we would consider as a good thing, but affliction is always good in the hands of our Creator (2 Cor. 4:17).

While we suffer through our afflictions, God is comforting us (2 Cor. 1:3). Psalm 56:8 tells us "you have kept count of my tossings, put my tears in your bottle. Are they not in your book?" God knows every tear that comes from us. He is with us as we enter the flames of affliction. He comforts us in ALL of our afflictions (2 Cor. 1:3). Not some of our afflictions. All of them. Every single trial, heartbreak, letdown, and persecution are all part of God's plan for our lives, and He is with us in every single one of them. Why would He be with us during these times? Why wouldn't He just take them away? It's simple. "*So that* we may be able to comfort those who are in any affliction, with the comfort with which we ourselves are comforted by God" (2 Cor. 1:4). God allows afflictions in our lives, but He doesn't leave us alone in them. He comforts us through them so that we can provide comfort to other people in our lives when they are experiencing the flames of affliction.

When God is in the classroom, this comfort in affliction is what

---

allows us to serve and follow Jesus. We can take the comfort that we receive from God through His son Jesus Christ, and give it to the least of these, our students. These children that have been entrusted to us come from many different backgrounds and walks of life. They experience many different trials at home and in the classroom. God has graciously given us all that we need in the death and resurrection of His Son and His Holy Spirit to comfort our students in their afflictions because He provides for us in our own afflictions. We are called to give this comfort to our students. Through Christ, we are to make it a point to form a relationship with our students. We are called to know and care about the trials they face so that when the time comes, we can give the true comfort to them that only comes from God.

APPLICATION: Read 2 Corinthians 1:3-11. Notice the depth of despair Paul felt in his affliction in Asia (vs. 9). Notice why these afflictions came to Paul. Write down this reason on a notecard. Keep the notecard handy. When you feel that your affliction is too much, read this card and rely on God to give you comfort. Then write down three ways you can give this comfort to your students.

GREATER THAN OURSELVES

By: Laura Ackley

MEMORY VERSES: "Do nothing from rivalry or conceit, but in humility count others more significant than yourselves. Let each of you look not only to his own interests, but also to the interests of others" (Phil. 2:3-4).

EXTENDED READING: Philippians 2: 1-18

No one has ever shown more humility than Christ Jesus. Before coming to the earth, Jesus was with God in Heaven—rich, exempt from pain and suffering. He was present at Creation and existed outside of time beforehand. He had power, authority, and wisdom beyond measure. And yet, despite any human logic that pleads for security and pleasure, Jesus "made Himself nothing, taking on the form of a servant, being born in the likeness of men, and being in human form, He humbled Himself by becoming obedient to the point of death, even death on a cross" (Phil. 2: 7-8). Why on earth would the One with the highest rank of exaltation subject Himself to such torment? The answer is very simple—He humbled Himself for our sakes—for the sake of the great love with which He has loved us.

Christ has proved that there is not a depth He will not endure for the sake of His beloved people. As we enter into our classrooms day after day, let us take a lesson from Jesus. Let us clothe ourselves in humility so that we will count the students and coworkers around us as more significant than ourselves. The goal is not to think less of ourselves; rather, the goal is to think of ourselves less as we fix our gaze upon Jesus' self-sacrificial love. As we consider the extravagant way in which Jesus prioritized us by being our Savior, we are able to focus less on our own interests and more on

---

the interests of others. Jesus' example to count other's as more significant than ourselves and to look to the interests of others is a call to "love [our] neighbor as ourselves" (Matt. 22:39).

This type of radical love is rare. Actually, it is downright impossible without Christ. Jesus calls us to change our perspective to making the good of others a priority. Sometimes this requires self-denial and sacrifice on our part, but in the end, we learn that there is reward in helping others. There is joy in putting to death our selfishness. Jesus' reward for considering our interests despite the personal cost is that He has been highly exalted and given the Name above every other name (Phil. 2:9). What will our reward be for sacrificing our time, energy, money, and more for the sake of our students' good? The Lord promises, "those who humble themselves will be exalted" (Luke 14:11). We are free to prioritize our students and coworkers, even when we feel they don't deserve our consideration, knowing that Jesus considered us worthy of His life. As we pour out our service for the good of others, we can know that "He who did not spare His own Son but gave Him up for us all, how will He not also with Him graciously give us all things" (Rom. 8:32).

APPLICATION: Ask the Holy Spirit to reveal to you three areas in your students' or coworkers' lives in which there is a need you can meet through your specific gifting, tools, time or resources, and then write them down. Read 1 John 3:17. Make a plan to practically meet the needs that you identified. Remember, as you show love and service to others, you are bringing glory to God, obeying God, and being used by God for good purposes. You are the hands and feet of Jesus. Wow, what a beautiful responsibility! If you won't help, who will?

THE CHALLENGE OF SANCTIFICATION

By: Briana Whistler

MEMORY VERSE: "Sanctify them in the truth; Your word is truth" (John 17:17).

EXTENDED READING: John 17:9, Philippians 2:13

The purpose of the Christian walk is to be made more into the image of God through a process called sanctification (2 Cor. 3:18). This means that we are made progressively more holy through obedience to God's truth that is only found in the Bible. By reading God's Word, we are opening ourselves up the sanctifying work of the Holy Spirit. God tells us that we are sanctified in the truth, and that His Word is truth (John 17:17). If we aren't reading God's truth, how can we expect to be sanctified through the Holy Spirit? And if the purpose of the Christian walk is to be made more in the image of God, how are we expecting to get there without knowing His truths?

Being conformed into the image of God's Son is part of God's plan for those who are in Christ (Rom. 8:29). It is a work that is done by the Holy Spirit, but we also have a part in it. We can only be sanctified because of God's grace and the Holy Spirit's work in our hearts, but we must do our part by opening ourselves up to truth that is only found in the Bible. We should make every effort to walk in obedience to Christ because we love Him (John 14:15), but if we don't know what Jesus commands from us how then can we walk in obedience? Sometimes this sanctification journey can lead us to trials of various kinds. How we respond to trials says a lot about our faith. Romans 5:2-5 tells us that "we rejoice in our hope of the glory of God. Not only that, but we rejoice in our sufferings, knowing that suffering produces endurance, and endurance produces character, and character produces hope, and hope does not put us to shame, because God's love has been poured into our hearts through the Holy Spirit who has been given to us." When we face a trial, rejoice in it, endure through it in obedience, grow in character, and cling to hope because the Holy Spirit is sanctifying us in our trial.

When God is in the classroom, this sanctification can look like many things. It could be drama with coworkers, enduring more work than you thought you were required to do, or even loving a student that challenges you in many ways. When we are faced with the challenge of a difficult student, we must first view this student as a child of God. This student is a born sinner, and God placed this student in our classroom for a reason. Cling to God's truth. Rejoice in the trial of this student being in our class. Endure the trial in obedience to Christ by reading the truth of God's word that helps us in our weaknesses. God will strengthen us for this task because He loves us enough to sanctify us through it. What a blessing that God would give us such a chance to grow our faith in Him!

APPLICATION: Read Philippians 2:12-18. How does Paul say we should respond in our trials? Who works in you and through you? Think of the students that require the most strength from you. Write down three reasons for each child that you are thankful for their presence in your classroom. Pray and thank God for each of these students.

THE POWER OF PRAYER

By: Laura Ackley

MEMORY VERSE: "And this is the confidence that we have toward Him, that if we ask anything according to His will He hears us" (1 John 5:14).

EXTENDED READING: Matthew 6:5-13, Philippians 4:6-7, Matthew 18:19-20

We are quick to neglect personal prayer as we busy ourselves with the happenings within our classrooms. While constant communication with Christ is ours through the gift of prayer, we tend to rely on our own efforts to solve problems. Sometimes, without conscience effort, we consider our work as more important than a pause to connect with Christ through prayer. Jesus, although possessing supreme power, prayed while carrying out His ministry on the earth. Often, He would steal away to quite places to pray for hours—usually in the middle of the night (Matt. 14:23). "Jesus Himself would often slip away to the wilderness and pray" (Luke 5:16). If Jesus needed to get alone with God and pray, how much more do men and women?

We do not know everything that Jesus prayed during His alone time with God, but we do know that He prayed over little children. In the midst of His teaching, when He was no doubt extremely busy and surrounded by a crowd that needed His teachings, parents were bringing their children to Jesus asking Him to pray for their kids. At first, the disciples rebuked the parents for disturbing Jesus' work, but Jesus said, "Let the little children come to me . . ." as "He laid His hands on them" to bless them (Matt. 19:13-15). Even now, Jesus lives to make intercession for those that draw near to God (Heb. 7:25). Jesus Christ is currently at the right hand of God, mediating for all of His people (Rom. 8:34). May we learn from His example of a prayerful life.

Christians are called to pray at all times in the Spirit (Eph. 6:18) and exhorted to "pray without ceasing" (1 Thess. 5:17). Why? Because we desperately need Him and so do our students. There are problems that we face that are beyond our control that we must take to the Lord in prayer. Prayer aligns our hearts with the will of God, helps us to resist temptation, and in prayer there are answers to be found. "The eyes of the Lord are on the righteous, and His ears are open to their prayer" (1 Pet. 3:12). When we draw near to God, we can count on the fact that we will find His grace to help us in the time of need. He hears from Heaven. He responds. Before we even cry out to Him, He hears. We must follow the example of Jesus when we are at our wits end and turn to Him in our distress through prayer. When we lack wisdom, we must cry to Him for help. We must remember to bring our anxious thoughts and our requests to God in prayer at all times. He is listening. He is in our classrooms.

APPLICATION: Today, carve out time to pray for each of your students by name. Whatever your concerns are, present them to God. Whatever you are thankful for, let the Lord be the first to hear.

ON PURPOSE
By: Briana Whistler

MEMORY VERSE: "Many are the plans in the mind of a man, but it is the purpose of the Lord that will stand" (Proverbs 19:21).

EXTENDED READING: Romans 8, Ecclesiastes 3:1-8, Psalm 16:5-6

Every day we make plans. Plans of where to eat, who to visit, what to do, etc. But what happens when our plans don't happen how we expected them to unfold? Maybe we didn't get picked, our car wouldn't start, or we were late for an event. Maybe we aren't where we expected ourselves to be when we made our plans in marriage, parenting, our career, or in our friendships. Plans fail, but God's purposes do not. His purposes will stand forever.

God is sovereign. This means that everything that happens in our lives has happened because He made it so. The good and the bad. He knew us before we were born (Ps. 139:13), and all of His plans for us are for good if we belong to Christ (Rom. 8:28). That doesn't mean they always feel good. In fact, some plans feel hard, or even impossible. These feelings stem from not trusting the Lord when He says that His plans for us are for good. We must trust His Word because His Word is truth (2 Tim. 3:16-17). Proverbs 3:5 tells us to "trust in the Lord with all your heart, and do not lean on your own understanding." Our understanding leads us to make our plans instead of seeking the purpose and path of God, but it is futile because the Lord's purpose will stand against any plans we make.

When God is in the classroom this means that each and everything that happens is part of His purpose. This includes us. We are part of God's purpose for our classrooms. God handpicked each person we would encounter- both student and coworker. He chose them for His sanctifying purposes and for building His Kingdom. The Lord's purpose will stand regardless of if we agree with it or not, but when we disagree

---

with God's purpose, we are complaining about God's plan for our lives and questioning His goodness. Today, be encouraged to embrace where you are, knowing that this is precisely where God planned for you to be. "But the plans of the LORD stand firm forever, the purposes of his heart through all generations" (Ps. 33:11).

APPLICATION: Read Psalm 16:11, Proverbs 4:11, and Acts 2:28. What do God's purposes lead you to? Write down three ways you can embrace God's purpose for your life. (Example: Pray for your coworkers/students.)

By: Briana Whistler

IT COUNTS FOR ALL ETERNITY

By: Laura Ackley

MEMORY VERSE: "Therefore, since we are surrounded by so great a cloud of witnesses, let us also lay aside every weight, and sin which clings so closely, and let us run with endurance the race that is set before us" (Heb. 12:1).

EXTENDED READING: 1 Corinthians 3:10-15

As teachers, we expend an incredible amount of energy seeking to meet the needs of others. We give our lives to ensure their well-being as thoughts of them consume our minds even after clocking out for the day. We care. Sometimes, when we just don't see the level of growth or accomplishment that we long to witness, it feels as if all of our efforts are in vain. The same is true relationally. We give of our hearts as we seek to help a child make a breakthrough in their behavior so that they will find success in school and life. Despite our support and counsel, it may seem as if nothing we say or do produces even the slightest inkling of change. At this point, discouragement sets in and we are left weary, burdened, and tempted to give up.

Despite our feelings, every amount of effort that we put forth for the betterment of others has eternal value. In 1 Corinthians 3, the Apostle Paul writes of the day in which Christians will stand before the Judgement Seat of Christ. Each Christian present at the Judgement Seat of Christ possesses the foundation of Salvation in Jesus Christ and has been spared the wrath of God against wickedness in Hell. Paul explains that Christians build upon their salvation with either gold, silver, precious stones, wood, hay, or straw. The gold, silver, and precious stones represent works done in Christlike faith and obedience. These materials stand in contrast to the wood, hay, or straw that represent sinful works and time wasted. As one stands before Christ, their works will be "revealed by fire" and "if the work that anyone has built on the foundation of Christ survives, he will receive a reward. If anyone's work is burned up, he will suffer loss, though he himself will be saved" (1 Cor. 3:10-15).

It is important to note that even though those who have put their faith and trust in Jesus Christ for Salvation have been spared from condemnation, they will in fact stand before the judge who will reward each according to the work that they carried out upon the earth in the name of Christ, for His glory, and for His Kingdom. The implication of such a truth is that each and every action or inaction counts for eternity. As we pour out in order to meet needs in the name of Christ, we are storing up eternal riches in Heaven. As we succumb to laziness, waste our lives on the couch, and fail to obey Christ, we must recognize that all we are amassing is hay, straw, and wood that will not matter when we stand before our King. May it never be so! May we be deeply encouraged by Jesus to run the race He has set before us with utter perseverance. May we run after Jesus as if to obtain a prize (1 Cor. 9:24). Through the grace of God, may we never forget that the entirety of our lives are lived out in His Presence, and nothing escapes His notice. He is in our classrooms. He is faithful to know, remember, and reward His faithful followers for their good works done in secret. Every ounce of effort we expend for the good of others counts for something.

APPLICATION: What are a few things you give time to that you know will be burned up when you stand before Christ? Maybe it's binge-watching TV or social media? Things that feel important on the earth may not be so when you stand before Jesus one day. What can you add into your life that is a precious stone, gold, or silver? Replace the chaff with something of eternal significance. Remember, if your heart is set on Christ, even sharpening pencils to His glory will be counted as gold when you stand before your Savior.

By: Laura Ackley

GOD'S VICTORY THROUGH JESUS

By: Briana Whistler

MEMORY VERSE: "He must increase, but I must decrease. He who comes from above is above all. He who is of earth belongs to the earth and speaks in an earthly way. He who comes from heaven is above all" (John 3:30-31).

EXTENDED READING: Psalm 3:8, 1 Corinthians 15:57, Proverbs 21:31

The Old Testament contains some of the greatest tales of battle. Time and time again God gave victory to His people, and time and time again His people turned from Him to go after the desires of their hearts. Some were even as bold as to take credit for their victories in battle. It's easy to hear of the Israelites and think that we would never do that, but how often do we give our victories to Jesus?

We have done nothing to be given the status as adopted children of God. The victory of our Salvation didn't come from us. It came at the mercy of a good and gracious God. Our salvation belongs to the Lord. Sin is defeated through the victory of Jesus Christ on the cross. This victory makes our small victories throughout our days seem trivial, but we must see that even our small victories belong to God. Proverbs 21:31 says, "The horse is made ready for the day of battle, but the victory belongs to the Lord". Every victory we have is because God gave it to us out of the abundance of His steadfast love. It is out of His omnipotence that we are given anything at all. It is important that God increase and that we would decrease. This doesn't mean that we think less of ourselves. It simply means that everything we do should be done to glorify God and increase Him among others. Our motives behind our actions are crucial when we think about God's victories. We must strive to not excel for our benefit and recognition, but instead to see each success as a wonderful blessing and a work of God in us. These successes in our lives belong to God.

When God is in the classroom, every victory belongs to Him. When a student excels, this is God's victory. When our day ends and we feel as though the day was a success, this is God's victory. Every moment of joy, excitement, praise, or love belong to the Lord. In those moments, stop and praise God for His sovereign control over our lives and for using us in a victory for His Kingdom.

APPLICATION: Read John 3:22-36. How does John exalt Christ? If anyone had a reason to feel success it was John the Baptist, yet he humbly gives the victory to Christ. Underline the top two verses that stand out to you in this account of humility. Pray and ask the Lord to help you walk humbly in His will, and to give each success to Him.

By: Briana Whistler

THE WORDS WE SPEAK
By: Laura Ackley

MEMORY VERSE: "Let no corrupting talk come out of your mouths, but only such as if good for building up, as fits the occasion, that it may give grace to those who hear" (Eph. 4:29).

EXTENDED READING: James 3:1-12, Ephesians 4:17-32

God is intimately acquainted with all our ways. Nothing we do, say, or think escapes His notice. In His infinite omniscience, His all-knowing character, He knows every word we will speak before it is even on our tongues (Ps. 139:4). Beyond that, He even knows our inner thoughts that we don't express aloud. He knows. Nothing is hidden from His sight, and He takes into account every word uttered from our mouths. If we are honest, we will admit that we speak words about our students, their parents, and coworkers that we would never say if Jesus stood before us in the flesh. The truth is that we are always in His presence. King David writes in Psalm 139, "Where shall I go from Your Spirit? Or where shall I flee from Your presence? If I ascend to Heaven, You are there! If I make my bed in Sheol, You are there" (vs. 8-9). We are prone to forget that we live our lives and speak our words in the presence of God at all times.

As Christians, we seek to bless the name of God with our words, but in the book of James, we find a sobering yet loving reminder about the hypocrisy of our words. "With [our words] we bless our Lord and Father, and with [our words] we curse people who are made in the likeness of God" (James 3:9). Each student in our classroom is a fellow image-bearer of God that should be spoken of in an honoring manner out of respect for the One in who's likeness they share. We find the willpower to use gracious words as sweet as honey when speaking about those in our care and those we work alongside as we recognize that we, too, have utterly fallen short of the glory of God. If people inspected our lives they would find things to

---

speak negatively about us as well; therefore, we choose to put a lid on the corrupting talk that threatens to spew out of our mouths, tear down others, and stir up anger. If we assume pridefully that we are religious, yet we fail to bridle our tongues, it is written that our "religion is worthless" (Jams. 1:26). Our words matter, and for them, we will give an account to God.

As we carry out our daily responsibilities, let us be encouraged by Jesus who said of Himself, "the words that I have spoken to you are spirit and life" (John 6:63). Through dependence on His Spirit, and remembrance of the words of life He has spoken to us, choose to give grace to those around by speaking words that build other people up. Today, we must choose to be the type of people who express themselves in a gracious matter knowing that we have been shown grace beyond measure by Jesus. Knowing that what comes out of our mouths started in our hearts, we must pray to God: "Let the words of my mouth and the meditation of my heart be acceptable in your sight, O LORD, my rock and my redeemer" (Ps. 19:14). God is in our classrooms, and our words matter to His heart.

APPLICATION: Choose several image-bearers of God that you have spoken about in a sinful manner. Then write down three ways in which you believe they need the blessing of God in their lives. Finally, take time praying on your knees for each of the people God put on your heart. Going forward, cling to the truth, "gracious words are like a honeycomb, sweetness to the soul and health to the body" (Prov. 16:24). It is for your good, and the good of others, and the glory of God that Jesus exhorts us to choose our words wisely.

COMMUNICATION IS CRUCIAL

By: Briana Whistler

MEMORY VERSE: "And this is the confidence that we have toward Him, that if we ask anything according to His will He hears us" (1 John 5:14).

EXTENDED READING: Matthew 26:41, James 5:13, Ephesians 6:18

Jesus said in John 14:15 "If you love me, you will keep my commandments." This means that we walk in obedience to the Lord because we love Him, not because we want something from Him. This is vital when we think about communication with God. The Bible is full of examples of people calling upon the name of the Lord. There are numerous scriptures where God commands us to communicate and pray. If we love Jesus, we need to make it a point to walk in obedience to Him with the command of communicating with Him.

Communication takes many forms. The easiest is prayer. We pray when we are happy, angry, sad, or joyful. God wants it all from us. One of the deepest prayers we can give is called a lament. David has filled the Psalms with these very prayers. A lament has four parts:

1. Address God (call Him Father or Lord).
2. Bring our burdens (tell Him how we feel and what we are carrying).
3. Boldly ask Him for His help (what do we need from Him).
4. Follow it all up with why we trust God through this storm. We must *always* land upon the truth of who God is. We trust Him because He is truly good (Romans 8 is a great resource on the goodness of God).

When God is in the classroom communication with Him can look like many things. Lamenting on a certain trial, praising Him for a blessing He has given, or even something as simple as a small breath prayer for strength. Breath prayers are short and simple, and we can say them within one breath. God just wants to hear us. And we know from 1 John 5:14, "that if we ask anything according to his will he hears us." God's will and not ours. We must talk to the Lord and keep Him at the forefront of our minds. We walk in obedience to Him and lay our victories and defeats at His feet.

APPLICATION: Read Psalm 145. Note the different forms of communication. Generations communicating with other generations, prayer, and praise. Write down three reasons to give praise to God today in your classroom.

UNWARRANTED PATIENCE

By: Laura Ackley

MEMORY VERSE: "But I received mercy for this reason, that in me, as the foremost, Jesus Christ might display His perfect patience as an example to those who were to believe in Him for eternal life" (1 Tim. 1:16).

EXTENDED READING: 1 Timothy 1: 12 -17

If anyone has the right give up on us, it is God. Often, even our best attempts to honor Him are tainted by our sinful actions, thoughts, and attitudes. We have utterly missed the mark of perfection even after experiencing His salvation. We are prone to wander and fall into sinful patterns that seem to be on repeat in our lives despite our best efforts. Oh, how desperately we need His mercy and forgiveness. Despite our failures, He doesn't grow irritable or resentful as we live imperfectly. In fact, His love is said to "endure all things" (1 Cor. 13:7). He bears with us in our failures because through Christ, He considers us His "chosen ones, holy and beloved" (Col. 3:12).

It is Jesus' nature to be patient towards us. He displays His perfect patience towards us because it is His heart's desire that none should perish, but that all would reach faith and repentance through a relationship with Him (2 Pet. 3:9). Sometimes in our weakness, we need the reminder that "Christ came into the world to save sinners" as we learn to depend on His sufficient grace and mercy (1 Tim. 1:15). We need to recognize that while we don't deserve His patience, He is "merciful and gracious, slow to anger and abounding in steadfast love" toward us (Ps. 103:8). Since He has freely lavished His patience and love upon us, we are beckoned by His power and through His Spirit to do the same for the students in our care.

Let's be honest, sometimes repeated misbehavior from students and/or coworkers causes sinful emotions to stir within us. Sometimes, these feelings boil over into our words and actions. In light of God's patience toward us, we are invited by Christ to choose humility. Instead of irritability towards those whose words and actions tempt us to forsake love, Jesus calls us to humble ourselves and remember how unbelievably patient He is with us in our own mess. In 1 Corinthians 13:5, the Apostle Paul writes, inspired by the Holy Spirit, that love is not irritable or resentful. When we begin to despise one in our care and find ourselves growing impatient toward their repeated misbehavior, there is only One to turn to in our struggle. Due to the constant gift of fellowship with Christ through His Spirit, each Christian has the ability to walk in the fruit of the Spirit—patience. As we experience temptation towards irritability, remember to cast your burdens on the Lord because He cares for you. If you ask Him, He will help you to love your students by operating in His patience. Has He not been infinitely patient with us when we deserve His wrath? As you choose to be patient with your students, know that you are manifesting the character of Christ in whom you abide to the world around you—specifically, your classroom.

APPLICATION: In the spirit of humility, make a list of each event that has caused you to react in impatience today. Read 1 John 1:9 and thank Him for His forgiveness. Then write down the top three circumstances that the enemy uses to tempt you toward impatience. In light of each circumstance listed, pray and ask the God of all patience to help you manifest His character in your specific circumstances for His glory and the good of all impacted.

                    By: Laura Ackley

PEACE THAT OVERCOMES
By: Briana Whistler

MEMORY VERSE: "I have said these things to you, that in Me you may have peace. In the world you will have tribulation. But take heart; I have overcome the world" (John 16:33).

EXTENDED READING: John 14:27, 2 Corinthians 4:17-18, Isaiah 26:3

Peace isn't a term normally associated with a classroom. The number of bodies in one room, noises, and movement all add to make the classroom a little less than peaceful. It's easy to be overwhelmed in the classroom. It's easier to be overwhelmed by the number of responsibilities that plague us every day outside of the classroom. From the many hats we wear, to the stress outside our jobs, to the weight of work expected within our jobs—it all adds up. By worldly standards we are stressed.

Oh sister, take heart! Jesus spoke of these very things to His disciples. "I have said these things to you, that you may have peace. In the world you will have tribulation. But take heart; I have overcome the world" (John 16:33). Satan wants us stressed because when we are in a state of turmoil it's easier to turn to sin to escape the pressure. Maybe its alcohol, books, movies or other activities that don't glorify the Lord. Maybe we are even tempted to escape from our responsibilities at home because of weariness. When we are experiencing tribulation or trials, our souls can go into a place of turmoil if we aren't focused on Jesus (1Pet. 5:8).

Jesus is our peace. He has overcome every single obstacle and trial we face. The weight of the world's sins was on His shoulders, and He took on God's wrath so that we might live in a state of peace with Him. Turn to Him! Reading His word, praying to Him, trusting Him through the hard things because we know He is good, and walking in obedience to His word because we love Him are all ways we can experience His

---

peace. But when we turn to our trials, and we dwell on our feelings of anger, depression, or anxiety we are opening ourselves up to the world of turmoil that Satan has invited us to (Rom. 8:5). Jesus is the Prince of peace, and He has extended an open invitation to us in every single moment when the turmoil threatens to pull us under. We must open the door to His heart of peace and allow Him to calm our storms.

APPLICATION: Make a list of responsibilities inside and outside of the classroom that are overwhelming you. (Example: too many students, my house is always dirty, etc.). Now, put a star next to the responsibilities that you can handle (such a cleaning your house), and circle the responsibilities that are out of your control. Each responsibility that is circled belongs to God. It is out of your control, and God has given it to you in His sovereignty. Read Colossians 3:23. Think about your motives behind each of your responsibilities and remember that even if you have a lot of things to do, you are to do everything for the Lord. Pray over your list and ask the Holy Spirit to help you work for the Lord and not for the world.

GUARD MY MOUTH
By: Laura Ackley

MEMORY VERSE: "If anyone thinks he is religious and does not bridle his tongue but deceives his heart, this person's religion is worthless" (James 1:26).

EXTENDED READING: Colossians 4:6, Proverbs 26:20-22, Matthew 7:1-5

Anytime people are together for a long period of time, gossip and slander are sure to be temptations. No one is perfect in regard to their speech, and no one is exempt from the harmful effects of being spoken about in a destructive manner. If we are honest, we will agree that there is something bad or negative that we could say about every person on the face of the earth. Every leader, teacher, parent, student, and pastor messes up—royally. It takes a courageous soul to choose a life that is characterized by speech that is honoring toward imperfect humans rather than engaging in gossip and slander. We must know we will not find peace or joy in gossip and slander—only suffering.

Everyone has fallen short when it comes to sins of the tongue. In fact, the apostle James writes that "no one can tame the tongue" and describes the tongue as "unrestrainable evil and full of deadly poison" (Jam. 3:7-8). Before we give up on the task of bridling our tongues, we must remember that when it comes to overcoming sinful patterns in our lives, "With men [it] is impossible, but with God all things are possible" (Matt. 19:26). We are commanded "to speak evil of no one, to avoid quarreling, to be gentle, and to show perfect courtesy toward all people" (Tit. 3:2). As we seek to bring glory to God with the way that we speak about children and adults alike, we must recognize that sanctification is a process. As we stumble and express ourselves in an ungodly manner, we do well to apologize to all people impacted by our words—listeners and victims alike.

We'd all agree that quarreling in the workplace is exhausting and negatively impacts those involved. Just like a fire would go out if there was a lack of wood, the quarreling would cease if the gossip ended (Prov. 26:20). Without being rude, we can wisely choose to spend less time with people who are constantly revealing secrets and downgrading others. Instead of engaging in conversations that tear down the students in our care, we can choose to embody the Light that points out the positive attributes in students. We are in fact told to think about things that are true, honorable, just, pure, lovely, commendable, excellent, and worthy of praise (Phil. 4:8). If we want to experience peace, we do well to mind our own business and seek peace through avoiding corrupting speech. As we face temptations to gossip and slander, may our earnest prayer be, "Set a guard, O Lord, over my mouth; keep watch over the door of my lips" (Ps. 141:3)! May our lives be characterized by gracious speech that leads to peace in our relationships as we choose to align our minds, words, and hearts with the will of God. As we choose words of truth and love, we remember, that God is in our classrooms.

APPLICATION: Journal a situation in which you have been the victim of gossip and slander. Then recount how many times you have been forgiven by God and how often sinful language has left your lips. Knowing how much you have been forgiven by Christ, release your hurt into the hands of Jesus and forgive from your heart. Next, consider who has been the victim of your gossip or slander. You never sin in a vacuum; therefore, the corrupting speech spoken has produced damage. Write down a couple of ways in which you can humbly make amends.

By: Laura Ackley

THE BIBLICAL PRINCIPLE OF REPLACEMENT

By: Briana Whistler

MEMORY VERSE: "Finally, brothers, whatever is true, whatever is honorable, whatever is just, whatever is pure, whatever is lovely, whatever is commendable, if there is any excellence, if there is anything worthy of praise, think about these things" (Phil. 4:8).

EXTENDED READING: Philippians 4

Paul told the church of Corinth to "take every thought captive and make it obedient to Christ" (2 Corinthians 10:5). Our thoughts are crucial to the state of our hearts. Proverbs 4:23 says to "guard your heart, for everything you do flows from it." If our thoughts contribute to what flows from our hearts, then it is imperative that we keep our thoughts in line with Christ.

When unrighteous thoughts enter our mind, we must take them captive using scriptures so that we are not being "conformed to this world" (Rom. 12:2). "All scripture is breathed out by God and profitable for teaching, for reproof, for correction, and for training in righteousness" (2 Tim. 3:16-17). To replace our thoughts, we must identify the unrighteous thought. Then we use our Bibles to see what God's truth tells us and "be transformed by the renewal of your mind" (Rom. 12:2). We must set our minds on things that are true, honorable, just, pure, lovely, commendable, excellent, and praiseworthy (Philippians 4:8). This use of thought replacement, or mind renewal, allows us to "set our hope fully on the grace that will be brought to us at the revelation of Jesus Christ" (1 Pet. 1:13). When we set our minds of this hope, "the God of peace will be with you" (Phil. 4:9).

When God is in the classroom, thought replacement is of the upmost importance. We are given countless opportunities to set our thoughts on our own selfish desires and feelings, but when we can renew these thoughts and make them obedient to Christ, we open ourselves up to the peace of God (Phil. 4:9) that can guard our hearts through our hope in Christ Jesus. When we have this peace, we can humbly walk in love amongst even the most challenging situations.

APPLICATION: Write down 5 unrighteous thoughts that you have had regarding your classroom, students, administration, or parents. Next, dive into the Bible and battle these thoughts with scripture to replace your thoughts and make them obedient to Christ. Pray that God will help you to walk humbly and renew you mind in your moments of unrighteousness.

By: Briana Whistler

Laura Ackley has been a Christian since 2004. She earned her master's degree in curriculum and instruction and is passionate about creating education and Bible study curriculum for the glory of God. In 2021, she had published a 20-week Bible Study named *YHWH, The LORD* that guides readers through a study of the infinite nature and character of God as revealed through His names. Laura served as an elementary public educator for five years before opening Mrs. Ackley's Adventure School—a Christian Pre-Kindergarten she has operated for the past three years. Within her local church, she serves as a worship leader, youth leader, Bible teacher at youth and women's events, and enjoys coordinating community outreach events. Laura is a wife to her high school sweetheart, Scott Ackley, and mother to two children: Kylie and Levi. Her hobbies include hiking, camping, animals, social gatherings, reading, singing, writing, public speaking, and coffee.

Briana Whistler began her journey as a follower of Christ in July of 2008. She serves as a kindergarten teacher in her hometown while running her own photography business. She is the author of *Little Tears, Great Counselor: When Sorrow Comes to Young Souls,* and has won Navarro County's Best of the Best Elementary School teacher in 2021 and 2022. She is happily married to her best friend and high school sweetheart. They have two growing in grace daughters they raise at their ranch home in Texas and one perfect son that lives in heaven with Jesus. She enjoys reading, writing, cozy fires, fuzzy socks, dogs, and coffee. Her love for her family and Christ has given her inspiration for writing books from which many families can benefit.

PREVIOUS PUBLICATIONS:

Briana Whistler published a children's book in 2021 designed for young souls that have experienced great sorrow in life titled *Little Tears, Great Counselor*. This book seeks to teach children about the Biblical concept of lament as they learn to speak to God about their sorrows. The book can be purchased through Amazon or the WestBow Press website.

Laura Ackley published through Equip Press an in-depth, 20 week adult Bible study titled *YHWH, The LORD* in 2021. In this study, readers are guided through Scripture surrounding ten different names ascribed to God throughout the Old Testament. This Bible study explores the infinite nature of God while beckoning readers toward a deeper, personal relationship with God. This Bible study can be purchased through any source that sells books online including Amazon, Walmart, and Barnes and Noble.

BIBLIOGRAPHY:

ESV Study Bible: English Standard Version, Wheaton, IL: Crossway, 2011.